Blueprint for a Self-Designed Life

A Discovery Guide for Your Ideal Life

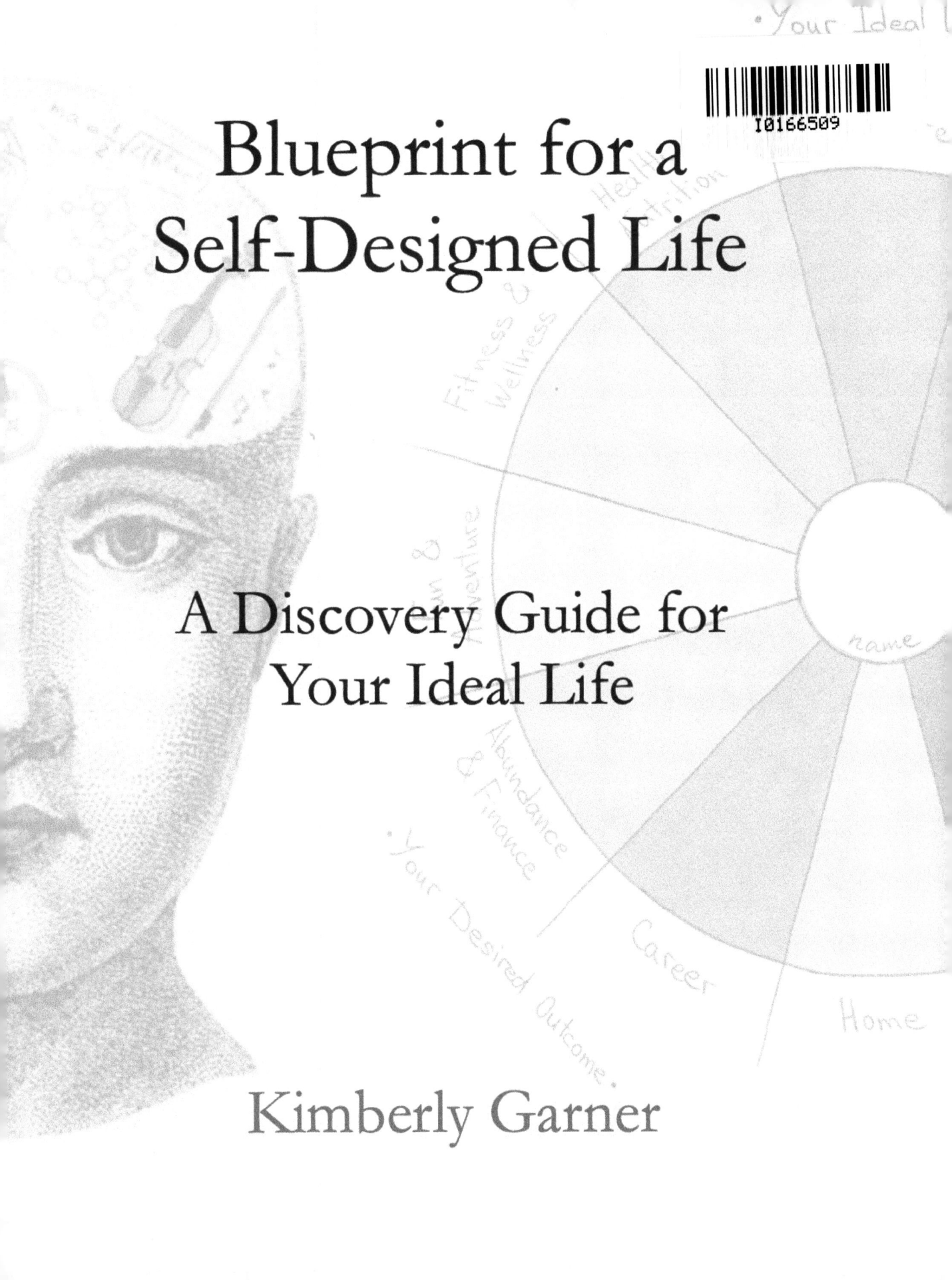

Kimberly Garner

Blueprint for a Self-Designed Life

A Discovery Guide for Your Ideal Life

Kimberly Garner

ISBN:978-1-951689-00-1

Table of Contents

Introduction

This guide was designed to reflect the process I use with my clients for clarifying the vision for their "ideal" life. Once identified, addressing and sorting through the obstacles blocking their intentions becomes quite clear. When we know what we're going after, we more effectively determine what's supporting our progress and what's getting in the way. Blueprint for a Self-Designed Life offers fabulous guidance for discovering what you desire, and even more importantly, the values behind your desire, so you are positioned to design your ideal life. (It's worth noting, when I use the term "ideal", I'm referring to YOUR version of ideal, not society, not your family or friends.) This guide is intended as a companion to the Blueprint course, but stands alone as a pivotal component to goal seeking endeavors. Blueprint for a Self-Designed Life offers the best tools I know for identifying and accelerating your intentions and desires.

Part One of this guide takes you through a strategic, thorough and fun process to draw out the themes you want most. Part Two is designed as your guide to address the myriad ways clutter shows up in your life. When you become aware of the far-reaching effects of clutter, you begin the process of alignment. Together we're going to explore clutter in your physical home, but also your internal home, the space of your mind. Consider this book your personal guide for initiating change towards the life you most desire.

We made a promise to ourselves about the future, the life we intended to live, and how our stories would unfold. Often our vision gets sidetracked. This guide is about you and only you. It's about accessing your truth and your vision for the life you most want. From there, we will clear the way of obstacles blocking your progress, so you're set on the trajectory of your choosing.

In order to get to where you want, we must focus your vision. Sometimes that, in and of itself, feels daunting. So we're going to go through a thorough and fun exploratory process. This is the first layer and step before we set your "house in order". We're getting the vision of your desires, intentions and values in order, everything grows from here. Each page is all about you and what you want. This step is instrumental and will inform how we'll move forward. Once your vision is clear, you'll be ready to implement the Holistic ID Room by Room Method.

Are you ready to explore answers to revealing questions and address what's blocking you from your desires?

I truly hope you enjoy your Holistic ID Blueprint Guide: Your Self Designed Life as much as I enjoyed creating it for you.

When you define your desires, intentions and values, you're exponentially more likely to achieve them. With the Holistic ID Method, everything flows from The Wheel. It's a fabulous tool for identifying where you are today and what needs to shift to make your day to day life feel better. Follow the instructions below and let's see where your life might need some bolstering and focus.

Your Holistic ID Wheel

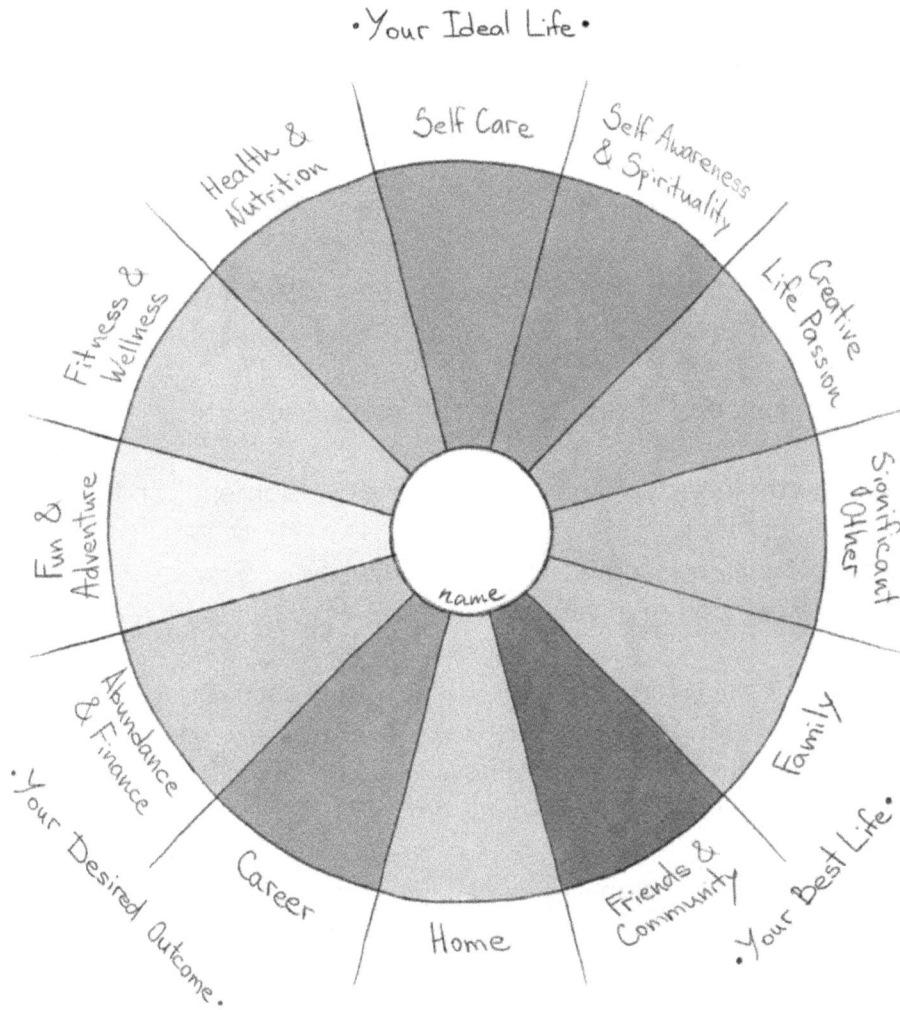

1. Review the 12 categories on your Holistic ID Wheel. We want the combination of categories to reflect the elements you require for a balanced and fulfilled life. If necessary you can split category segments to add in something you feel missing, or rename an area to make it more meaningful for you.

   HERE ARE SOME EXAMPLES:

   Family and Friends: Split "Family and Friends" into separate categories if you feel each needs differing attention. May also include "Community".

   Significant Other: Includes "Dating", "Marriage", "Relationship" or "Life Partner".

   Career: Includes "Motherhood", "Work", "Business" or "Volunteering".

   Finances: Includes "Money", "Prosperity" or "Financial Wellbeing".

   Health: Includes "Emotional", "Physical", "Fitness", "Spiritual" or "Well-being".

   Home Environment: Add "Physical Environment" if your geographic location feels important for balance and well-being.

   Fun & Leisure: Includes "Travel", "Recreation" or "Adventure".

   Personal Growth: Includes "Learning", "Self-Development" or "Spirituality"

   Other categories to add could include "Security", "Service", "Leadership", "Achievement" or "Community".

2. Now think about your version of the ideal within each category of your life. What would a "10" look and feel like? This is your metric. Your personal ideals guide this exercise. Quiet the external voices of how "success" should look. Expand your experience of what and how a "10" would feel for YOU.

3. Rank your level of satisfaction based on where you are today within each category of your life. Place a value between 1 (very unfulfilled) and 10 (extremely fulfilled) within each category segment, write the number reflecting your fulfillment within each category of your life and draw a line bisecting the category wedge.

4. The new perimeter of the circle represents your Holistic ID Wheel. The wheel helps you tap into where you are today as far as your level of satisfaction within each area and offers a new perspective to explore where you want to go. Your awareness will lead to the change you seek.

Your Holistic ID Wheel

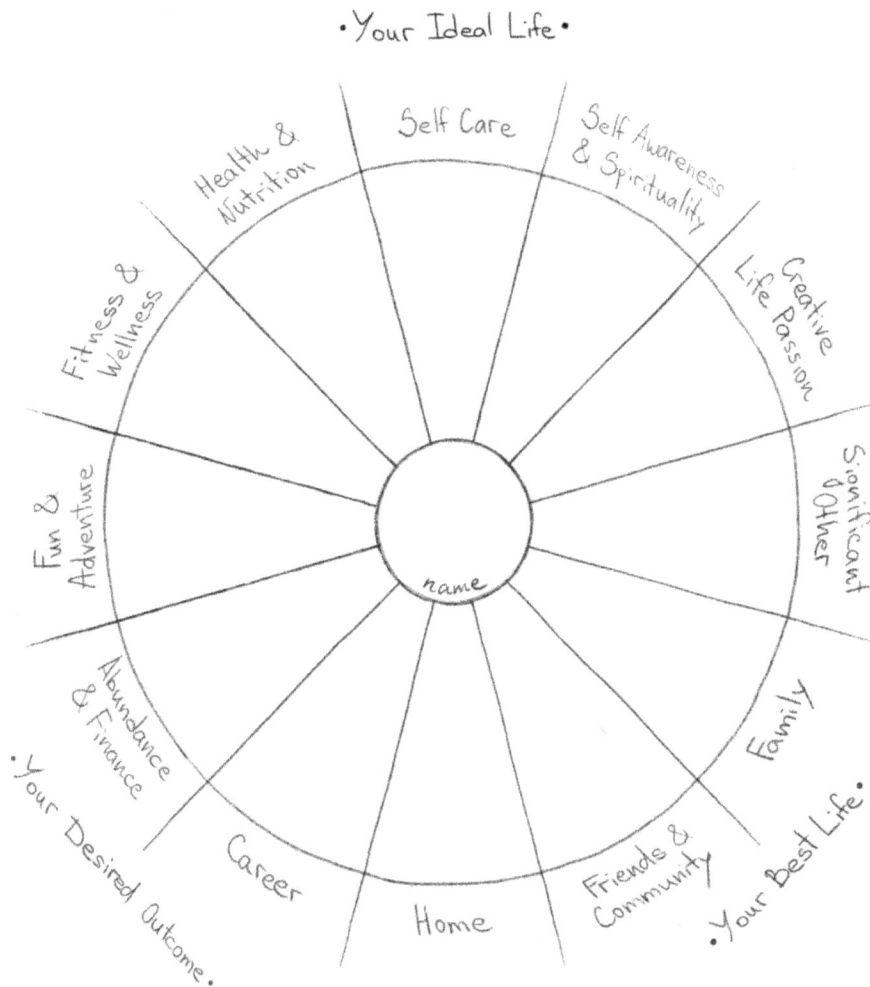

· Your Ideal Life ·

Self Care

Self Awareness & Spirituality

Health & Nutrition

Creative Life Passion

Fitness & Wellness

Significant Other

Fun & Adventure

name

Family

Abundance & Finance

· Your Best Life ·

· Your Desired Outcome ·

Career

Home

Friends & Community

Your Life Drivers: Let's focus on the three key areas of your life where you're seeking some level of change. Using the information from your Holistic ID Wheel, which 3 sections/life aspects, if changed today to a "10" would make the biggest impact on your life and well-being?

1.

2.

3.

What 3 actions might you take to move closer towards your version of a "10" within these three areas?

Actionable items:

_____

_____

_____

_____

Actionable items:

_____

_____

_____

_____

Actionable items:

_____

_____

_____

_____

Notes:

Your Board of Directors: Did you know you have a personal Board of Directors available to you at all times, any hour, any day, holidays included? It's true. These three people are POWERFUL allies, they've known you your entire life, they know you better than anyone else on the planet. Whenever you find yourself in a tough mental or emotional place, seek counsel here first. You'll be surprised at how much they've got your best interest at heart, and their counsel is potent, loving and wise. Meet your Board of Directors:

Your Innocent Younger Self: This is the loving, innocent and imaginative part of your nature and reflects who you were as a five or six year old child. Consider what this child might share with you about you and your life as it is today. Consider the clarity and the wisdom this child holds through the purity of being, seeing and engaging in the world. They possess a perspective we've very likely lost sight of as we've "grown up".

Your Wise Older Self: This is the wise, loving and compassionate version of yourself you haven't grown into just yet. They know ALL of your stories, all of your insecurities and they have witnessed you and your strengths all along. This is your inner 85-year-old. Consider the grace and wisdom they've acquired through the tragedies and triumphs of life. Their perspective is unique and priceless.

Your Future Self: Ahhh, the future version of you! This is your potential amplified. This is who you are and how you were born to live on this planet. This is the version of yourself beyond what you dreamed possible. This version of yourself is graceful and aware of the power you carry. You are your future self. Tap into this aspect of yourself and get curious as to how they might guide you. Your Future Self knows what you're capable of and holds the mirror up for your greatness better than anyone.

Take these relationships with you as you delve into your loftiest intentions, your biggest dreams and make sure to bring them along during the challenges. They know how to support you and keep you on track. Keep your Board of Directors close.

Interview your Board of Directors:

Interview your Younger Self:

Imagine yourself as a 5 or 6 year old. If you had a conversation with this version of you, what would they have to say about your life, your choices, your habits, routines, and your well-being?

Describe them?

_____

_____

_____

_____

How do they carry themselves?

_____

_____

_____

_____

Describe what their life feels like.

What does a day in their life look like?

What do they enjoy?

What do they do for fun?

_____

_____

_____

_____

How do they spend their alone time?

_____

_____

_____

_____

What are some of their favorite things to do?

_____

_____

_____

_____

What do they want you to know about yourself?

What do they want to tell you about your life?

What do they want for you?

How would they ask you to live, behave, speak, and spend your free time?

_____

_____

_____

_____

_____

Do they have any concerns about you and your life?

_____

_____

_____

_____

_____

Interview with your Future Self: Imagine your ideal self, 5 to 10 years from now. You're living your best life on all levels. If this version of you were here, and you got to have a conversation about that life (your future life waiting for you), how would it differ from your current life, your choices, your habits and routines, your well-being, and what would they likely say?

Describe them.

How do they carry themselves?

Describe what their life feels like.

What does a day in their life look like?

What do they enjoy?

What do they do for fun?

How do they spend their alone time?

What are some of their favorite things to do?

What do they want you to know about yourself?

What do they want to tell you about your life?

What do they want for you?

How would they ask you to live, behave, speak, spend your free time?

Do they have any concerns about you and your life?

_____

_____

_____

_____

_____

Notes:

_____

_____

_____

_____

_____

_____

_____

_____

_____

_____

_____

Interview your Older Wiser Self: Imagine yourself at 80-85 year old self, you've got the wisdom of time on your side and the benefit of hindsight. Imagine this version of you were here to share a conversation with you.

What would they like to share about your life, your choices, your habits, routines, and your well-being?

What do they want you to know about yourself?

What do they want to tell you about your life?

What do they want for you?

_____

_____

_____

_____

How would they ask you to live, behave, speak, spend your free time?

_____

_____

_____

_____

Do they have any concerns about you and your life?

_____

_____

_____

_____

Your Fairy Godmother

I magine that your fairy godmother just arrived and wants to grant you ANY three wishes. It's a big task considering what to ask for when given the opportunity. Many times our initial reaction is what society or our culture tells us to want, but deep down, is that **really** what we want? Now here's the thing, if we aren't clear about exactly what we want, then what are we doing with our precious time and in what direction are we focusing our energy?

Take some time to think about this scenario, then write down your three wishes: Hint (You may want to consult your Personal Board of Directors for this exercise. What would your inner child, elder self and future self encourage you to wish for?)

P.S. You're not allowed to wish for another wish ;)

"You must ask for what you really want." -Rumi

1.

2.

_____

_____

_____

_____

3.

_____

_____

_____

_____

Circle the areas your three wishes relate to:

Self-Care   Life Work/Career

Self Growth/Spirituality   Prosperity/Finance

Creativity/Life Passion   Adventure/Fun

Intimacy/Significant Other   Fitness/Physicality

Family   Vitality/Health

Community/Friends   Other_____

Physical Environment/Home

Now let's imagine your 3 wishes have been granted. You're living your life from a place with your wishes actualized.

How do you feel different with these wishes actualized?

How do you feel about yourself and your life?

How will you spend your time, days, seasons, and years from this place of actualized wishes?

Looking at your responses from the last two sections, list below all the values, themes or connections you notice coming up:

_____

_____

_____

_____

_____

Your Big Road Trip

I f you decided to take a road trip, would you get in the car and just start driving without a direction, plan or your various destinations mapped out? No, you wouldn't. You'd likely spend a certain amount of time planning, organizing, and packing before you head out on your adventure. So why would how you live your life be any different?

Not identifying your desires, intentions and values is like going on a road trip without choosing a direction or destination. If you haven't defined where you're going, it's unlikely you'll get there.

Your BIG Life Road Trip

• Where do you want to go (in your life)?

_____

_____

_____

_____

_____

_____

• What do you want to experience?

_____

_____

_____

_____

• Who would you like to share time with along the way?

_____

_____

_____

_____

• What kind of people would you like to meet and spend your time with?

_____

_____

_____

_____

• What things do you need to get you where you want to go or want to experience?

_____

_____

_____

_____

• What would you like to bring along? What do you love and will remind you of who you are and where you're going?

_____

_____

_____

_____

• What will make your trip/life run smoother?

_____

_____

_____

_____

• What stops and excursions or experiences would you like along your way?

_____

_____

_____

_____

• What's essential to your journey? What's not essential?

_____

_____

_____

_____

We must define our dreams and desires if we want to live them.

You've Just Won the Lottery!!

Congratulations! Whether you played or not, you've just won the lottery. List all the things you plan to do, buy, and experience now that you have complete financial freedom. You may need more space for this exercise. Feel free to staple or paperclip additional pages to this section.

Notes:

Once you've exhausted all the things you'll do with your new financial freedom, describe what a day in your life looks like after you've bought, traveled and experienced all you desire. How do you wake up? How does your morning look? How do your days unfold? What's your routine? What makes you most happy with your new life? Who are your people?

Notes:

Looking at your Lottery answers, list below all the values, themes or items you notice coming up:

Notes:

9 Lives: Imagine you're given 9 lives, name the career or vocation you would enjoy experiencing for each life.

1. _____

2. _____

3. _____

4. _____

5. _____

6. _____

7. _____

8. _____

9. _____

Notes:

The Best Things in Life Are Free.

Truly the best things in life are free. It's really powerful to consider the things in life that bring us wonder and joy and how many of those things are free. List all of the things in your life you cherish and value that come with zero financial expense. I'll start you off and share some of the universal freebies...rainbows, laughter, sunrises and sunsets...Also consider your Board of Directors, what would your Innocent Self, your Older Self, and your Future Self share? What are your favorite things that connect you to the truest essence of who you are and that bring you delight, peace, awe and wonder?

Your Time:

What are 10 things you love to do?

1. _____

2. _____

3. _____

4. _____

5. _____

6. _____

7. _____

8. _____

9. _____

10. _____

What are 3 things you'd like to incorporate in your daily routine?

1.

2.

3.

If I had everything I've ever wanted, this is how would I spend my day?

When I have "free" time for myself, I like to:

Notes:

The Red Thread

We each have an underlying theme inspiring and connecting all we do, this is our red thread.

Looking back at each exercise, highlight or circle words, values and themes that stand out most for you. This collection of words and themes give you an idea of your driving values. Write down those words, aspects or themes that stand out most from each exercise:

These aspects, words, and themes are your drivers, your values and they create the thread weaving your story, your life, and your moments. We will carry this narrative throughout the space of your home, room by room, so keep this journal in a safe place...it will serve as your manifesto as you move deeper into your home and your Holistic ID.

Your home is your living vision board:

What does it speak? Does it speak to your desires, values and intentions? Is it speaking to an outdated version of you or a version others expect? Does your home speak to who you truly are, your values, intentions, desires and dreams? Your home wants to reflect and hold up the mirror for you so you're continuously supported, reminded of who you are and the life you're actively creating. Is your home reinforcing your past or is it reshaping your future, the future aligned with what you most desire?

Describe the life you're actively creating:

Notes:

Your Desires

Considering the Holistic ID Wheel and Your Board of Directors (your Future Self, your inner younger self, and your wise older self), let's take a deeper look at your desires for each of the following areas. We're going to look at what your unique version of a "10" looks like and what you can do to move your life closer to your "10"? For each of the following areas, start to explore and identify your intentions and desires. Have fun with this section, push the boundaries of logic, social norms and previous stories or expectations. This is where you get to choose...and here's a hint, follow what gets you excited...imagine your desires in fruition and how good it feels...follow the feelings that light you up, you living your life your way.

You get to choose.

Health and Vitality: Your vitality feeds all aspects of your life. Without radiant vitality, everything else in your world exists under a muted veil. How do you want to physically feel? What's your ideal version of vitality and health? How does vitality look for you personally? How will a "10" vitality feel? What are the habits you want to adopt? How would you feel maintaining this version of you?

Desires & Intentions:

_____

_____

_____

_____

_____

What does a "10" look like?

_____

_____

_____

_____

What actionable steps might you take to move your life closer to your "10"?

_____

_____

_____

_____

Notes:

_____

_____

_____

_____

_____

Relationship and Romance Desires & Intentions:

We all want to feel fully loved for who we are, as we are. Our insecurities show up in relationships... it's really tender and vulnerable terrain, but that's why it's so rewarding and at its best, feels so good. How do you want to experience love with another? How do you want to communicate in your relationships? How would your highest experience of love serve your life and yourself? What do you want for yourself in a relationship with another? It's fun to get really specific here and whether you're in a relationship or single, there's fertile information here.

Desires & Intentions:

_____

_____

_____

_____

_____

_____

What does a "10" look like?

_____

_____

_____

_____

_____

What actionable steps might you take to move your life closer to your "10"?

Notes:

Financial and Abundance Desires:

This one is tricky! Society has us believing more and bigger is better, but listen to your inner voice, the voices of your Board of Directors: What's essential? What's too much? What's not enough? What do you want for yourself and your version of your best life? Is it the bigger house, the fancier car, the more exotic vacation? Maybe? Only you know. Take a moment to ask the question and listen beyond your ego for an answer.

Desires

What does a "10" look like?

What actionable steps might you take to move your life closer to your "10"?

Notes:

Work and Career Desires:

This one can be so tough. We're taught to grow up and join the "real world", act like an adult. What does that even mean?! Does it mean set your dreams and passions on the sideline and work a job that siphons your enthusiasm and zest for life? NOOOOO!!!

What's your passion? What do you consider your Life's Work? What are your talents & what do you love? Can these two be intertwined to create your life's work? Sometimes we must do our "survival" work to support our "spirit or soul work". If you're not creating an income from your soul work, what elements that stir passion in you can you bring to your current line of work? Just tapping into the delight of fully being yourself is passionate life "work". Look at your current line of work and how you might enhance your experience or take steps toward your dream job. Marry what you love with what comes easily and naturally for you.

Desires

_____

_____

_____

_____

What does a "10" look like?

_____

_____

_____

_____

What actionable steps might you take to move your life closer to your "10"?

Notes:

Fun and Adventure Desires:

What do you do for fun? Do you make time to play every day? What do you do that you just love? How do you enjoy spending your free time? Where do you find your delight? Where do you lose track of time because you're so caught up in the moment? We are meant to play and have fun... especially as adults. Why would anyone want to "grow up" if by default that meant no more fun, no more playing? Make play and fun more of a priority for your life. Hunt delight!

Desires & Intentions:

What does a "10" look like?

What actionable steps might you take to move your life closer to your "10"?

Notes:

Friends and Community Desires:

Who are your people, the inner circle of people who know you best and you consider yourself at home when you're with them? I call these people my first string. Sometimes this is one person, sometimes it's a handful of friends. How would you like your community and friendships to grow? What activities would you like to routinely engage in with others? What kind of moments would you like to create? How do you express your care and gratitude for others? How would you like to participate in the community? Do you prefer one on one or large groups?

Desires

What does a "10" look like?

What actionable steps might you take to move your life closer to your "10"?

Notes:

Family Desires:

Considering your version of family, how would you like to experience a more fulfilling family? Whether you have children or parents or siblings doesn't matter. We each have a family we were born into or have chosen throughout our life. The people we feel most "at home" with in the world are our family.

Where is there room to enhance your experience of family? What memories would you like to create for you and your family? What elements need nurturing? What could bring more balance into your family? Are there things that need to be said or things that do not need to be spoken?

Desires

_____

_____

_____

_____

What does a "10" look like?

_____

_____

_____

_____

What actionable steps might you take to move your life closer to your "10"?

Notes:

Self-Care & Self Knowledge Desires:

How do you take care of your body, mind and spirit? How you take care of your needs is primary. If you do not take care of your needs, whether it's body, mind, or spirit, you cannot attract the goodness and opportunities you deserve, quite simply, you cannot thrive. Once you care for yourself, life begins to reflect that care back to you in myriad ways.

What do you want? "What does __(your name here)__ want? What do you need more of in your life for you, your body, & spirit? What can you do to bring better balance to your life?

"Whatever the soul is, it's fed by things which honor its presence." Coleman Barks

Desires

_____

_____

_____

_____

_____

What does a "10" look like?

_____

_____

_____

_____

_____

What actionable steps might you take to move your life closer to your "10"?

_____

_____

_____

_____

_____

_____

_____

Notes:

_____

_____

_____

_____

_____

_____

_____

Home & Physical Environment Desires:

How do you like your home? How do you like your neighborhood, city, region, or geographical area? If you could live anywhere, where would you live? What would your home be like? Use the space below to clarify that which you most want for your home and physical environment. Where we live affects how we live and experience life. Think broadly and be descriptive when defining your intentions and desires. What landscapes feel like home to you? Mountains, rolling hills, the sea, the ocean, the prairie, the city? Explore your personal sense of place and what it means for you to be home.

Desires

What does a "10" look like?

What actionable steps might you take to move your life closer to your "10"?

Notes:

PART 2: OBSTACLES & CLUTTER

Now it's time to look at the obstacles holding you back, the clutter blocking your well-intended desires and intentions! The Holistic ID definition of clutter is a little different from the standard definition. Moving forward, use this concept of clutter as you move throughout your home and your life:

Clutter is any obstacle which blocks or distracts your dreams, desires, intentions and overall well-being. It is any single thing that gets in the way of what you most want, no matter what form it takes.

There are 3 primary categories of Clutter:

Physical Clutter: The objects & items in our physical environment (our home, car, office, etc.) that distract or in any way undermine our values, desires and intentions.

Emotional Clutter: The feelings, old stories, or beliefs that distract or in any way undermine our peace of mind, well-being, sense of self and block us from our values, desires, and intentions.

Mental Clutter: The thoughts, inner chatter, preoccupations of the mind that consume us and distract us from our life and how we want to live. Like emotional clutter, it undermines our peace of mind, well-being and blocks our values, desires and intentions.

Clutter keeps us focused on what we don't want and blocks the vision of our dreams.

5 SUBCATEGORIES OF CLUTTER:

Verbal Clutter: The words we choose, the language we speak, the tone we use aloud and within our thoughts which undermine what we want and are in contradiction to our values, intentions and desires.

Time Clutter: The time we occupy which is not aligned with our values, desires and intentions. It's important to look at how we habitually spend our time and what's become routine, unnecessary and an unproductive distraction from what we ultimately desire..

Relationship Clutter: The relationships and perspectives we hold within our relationships which make us small, do not serve our values or desires, and feel unhealthy or unaligned.

Financial Clutter: The beliefs and behaviors which are unaligned with our desires, values or intentions.

Vitality Clutter: The choices and behaviors which do not align with supporting, feeding and promoting the vitality we desire and intend for ourselves and our life.

The Holistic ID Litmus Test for Clutter

Do you love it?

Do you use it?

Does it support your desires, values and intentions?

Take a look around your home. Do your belongings pass the Holistic ID Litmus Test?

Imagine loving everything throughout your home, your space fully supporting your lifestyle, desires and values, while feeling empowered and inspired by your surroundings? How might your life be different if your home supported you at this level? It's fully possible and can impact your life in profound and exciting ways. Working through our clutter will bring us closer to experiencing "dwell-being" within our home.

Now consider how clutter shows up in other areas of your life (Emotional, Mental, Verbal, Time, Relational, Financial, Vitality).

Further questions to consider when determining clutter obstacles;

Do I consider this item to be something that supports my growth? Does this item help me avoid or protect myself from potentially undesirable outcomes? Avoiding something is based in fear. It's important to look at your choices in these terms. If you find yourself protecting or avoiding, you're letting fear lead your decisions, behaviors, actions, which ultimately affect your life. It's like resisting life and the possibilities available. When we behave in ways that support our adventure, we move toward our potential, our intended life, the life we were born to experience.

When considering the obstacles showing up in your life, ask yourself, is this thing (item, feeling, thought, relationship, choice) aligned with my values, intentions and desires?

Is this essential or necessary to the path I'm creating and the life I desire?

It's impossible to have clarity about your life when you're overwhelmed by any form of clutter.

When you say "yes" to something, by default, you're saying "no" to something else. So it's important to be clear about the items in your space and the choices in your life. Look at how you spend your days...what do you say "yes" to? What do you say "no" to?

What am I saying "NO" to? When you say "NO!" to clutter, you're saying "no" to: stagnation, distraction, frustration, constriction, lethargy, indecision, confusion, fear, protection, extra weight, congestion, procrastination, depression, disharmony, putting dreams on hold, disorganization, living in the past and more!

- What do you want to say "NO!" to?

- Considering the various types of clutter in your life (physical, mental, emotional, verbal, relational, time, financial, vitality), what things, thoughts, feelings, language, people, moments, choices do not serve your dreams and the vision you have for your future life?

- What are you ready to release today to make room for the opportunities of tomorrow?

- What things don't serve you, but might take a bit more time to release?

What am I saying "YES" to?

When you say "yes" to your dreams and desires, you're saying "yes" to: opportunities, vitality, clarity, love, growth, health, more free time, productivity, enthusiasm, efficiency, flow, peace of mind, the present moment and so much more.

What do you want more of in your life? What do you want to say "yes" to?

_____

_____

_____

_____

_____

Language of a thing:

Every item in your home has an associative and subjective thought, memory or feeling connected to it. Each of those items has a positive, negative or neutral effect and your job is to discern which objects are creating the undesirable mental and emotional response so you can remove them from your space.

Consider the items in your home and the language these objects speak. Make a list of each room in your home. Walk into each room and identify one object that stands out the most or holds the strongest "voice". What does this item speak? Is it positive, negative or neutral?

_____

_____

_____

_____

_____

_____

Possession vs. Belonging:

Look at each of these words and consider how they show up in your life. Journal about what "possession" means to you. Next, journal about what "belonging" means to you. Do you want your home to be filled with possessions or belongings? (I know, it's a loaded question!)

TOXIC CLUTTER:

Any single object in your home that brings up negative thoughts, feelings or memory is toxic clutter and must be removed from view, if not entirely removed from your home. Do you have an object in your home which brings up negative thoughts, feelings or memory? What is this item? What feeling or thought comes up in relation to this item? If it had a voice, what would it say? Why are you holding on to it? Are you willing to let it go? If not, why?

Feedback Loop:

Your subconscious is tightly interconnected with your physical environment and locks into a feedback loop when it comes into sensuous (relating to the five senses) contact with various objects in your home. You see something, the subconscious triggers a thought, and your thought becomes a feeling, which influences your mood, your attitude, which shifts your behavior, which shapes your routine, which over time becomes your habit, which ultimately creates the quality of your life.

"Your habitat becomes your habit."
Dr. Joe Dispenza

How does your home feel?

Make a list of each room. Sit in the room and describe how you feel in the room. Is it positive or negative? Describe what feels right and what feels out of sync.

"Your environment creates your mind."
Dr. Joe Dispenza

PHYSICAL CLUTTER

Where does physical clutter show up in your home?

_____

_____

_____

_____

Where is clutter most prominent in your home? How do you feel in this room?

_____

_____

_____

_____

Where is clutter the least prominent? How do you feel in this room?

_____

_____

_____

_____

By allowing clutter to coexist in your home, what are you saying "yes" to? What are you saying "no" to?

By removing clutter, what are you saying "yes" to? What are you saying "no" to?

Are you willing to set aside 15 minutes a day, a few days a week to address the clutter in your home? This is an act of self care, self devotion and self love. Write down below how you'll create time and space for addressing the clutter influencing your life. This is not a chore, it's a choice. You're choosing you.

Describe what you're actively making room for in your life by removing the clutter in your home. It could be peace of mind or it might be something of functional benefit, or something different altogether. The important thing is for you to be working toward an outcome you find personally rewarding. "By clearing the clutter from my_____, I'm creating_____which will help me_____."

MENTAL CLUTTER:

How does mental clutter show up in your life?

_____

_____

_____

_____

By focusing on these things, what are you saying "yes" to? "no" to?

_____

_____

_____

_____

Our self imposed misery lives in the gap between behaviors and values, the bigger the gap, the greater the discomfort. Where might your mental choice be unaligned with your values?

_____

_____

_____

In observing your thoughts, how is your mind preoccupied? List the recordings that play over in your mind that get in the way of achieving your goals or are not serving or supporting your values, desires and intentions:

1. Self-Care

2. Self Growth/Spirituality

3. Creativity/Life Passion

4. Intimacy/Significant Other

5. Family

6. Community/Friends

7. Physical Environment/Home

8. Life Work/Career

9. Prosperity/Finance

10. Adventure/Fun

11. Fitness/Physicality

12. Vitality/Health

List 10 thoughts that are aligned with that which you most want (these could be existing thoughts or thoughts you're ready to begin thinking today).

1.

2.

3.

4.

5.

6.

7.

8.

9.

10.

Notes:

EMOTIONAL CLUTTER:

How does emotional clutter show up in your life?

_____

_____

_____

_____

What feelings, beliefs or stories do you tell yourself that might be untrue?

_____

_____

_____

_____

How do your emotions get in the way of your desires, values and intentions?

_____

_____

_____

_____

How do you get emotionally hijacked?

_____

_____

_____

_____

What feelings, beliefs or stories are aligned with your desires and intentions?

_____

_____

_____

_____

"What you think about, you bring about."
~Bob Proctor

How do you feel about each area & what beliefs or stories do you tell yourself about your:

Self-Growth/Spirituality   Life Work/Career

Creativity/Life Passion   Prosperity/Finance

Intimacy/Significant Other   Adventure/Fun

Family   Fitness/Physicality

Community/Friends   Vitality/Health

Physical Environment/Home

Notes:

VERBAL CLUTTER:

How does verbal clutter show up in your life?

_____

_____

_____

_____

What language do you communicate with yourself or others that might be untrue or in contradiction to what you want?

_____

_____

_____

_____

How do your words get in the way of your desires, values and intentions?

_____

_____

_____

_____

What words or statements are aligned with your desires and intentions?

_____

_____

_____

_____

"Never finish a negative statement about yourself or your life."
~Joseph Murphy

Observe the words you speak and think.

Make a list of things you say which are not in alignment with your values, desires and intentions. They might start with "I'll never...Pay particular attention to words like "should, have to, never, always"

_____

_____

_____

_____

What is your Self-Talk? How do you speak to yourself in the quiet of your mind?

_____

_____

_____

_____

Are your statements True or Untrue?

Are you intentional or haphazard with your choice of language & words?

Notes:

What words do you speak about:

Self-Care

Self Growth/Spirituality

Creativity/Life Passion

Intimacy/Significant Other

Family

Community/Friends

Physical Environment/Home

Life Work/Career

Prosperity/Finance

Adventure/Fun

Fitness/Physicality

Vitality/Health

Notes:

RELATIONSHIP CLUTTER:

How does relationship clutter show up in my life?

_____

_____

_____

_____

Which relationships fill you up?

_____

_____

_____

_____

Which relationships deplete or leave you feeling small?

_____

_____

_____

_____

List your first string of peeps and why they make the team.

Consider the people who deplete you, is it time for a change?

Surround yourself with people who reflect more of what you want and align with your highest values.

Do you continue to put energy into relationships that make you feel small?

Do you need to create boundaries that honor your time and self-worth?

What do you want? What kind of person do you want to spend your time with?

Do you settle for bad love over no love? When we allow certain relationships to continue which don't serve our highest self, we're not allowing space for new opportunities or relationships to enter our lives.

*"When one **door** of happiness closes, another opens; but often we look so long at the closed **door** that we do not see the one which has been opened for us."*
- Helen Keller

*Remember our relationships are our greatest teachers, they teach us how to love, but even more importantly they teach us how to love our self. It's vital we recognize we are responsible for how we experience relationship with another. The other is often bringing up something we must learn and heal in order to grow, become emotionally sovereign. Be accountable in your relationships. When there's discomfort, ask yourself, "what is this situation offering me? What might I learn about myself and my own fear or inner pain that is being triggered right now? If we just point fingers and play the victim, we miss the true opportunity. Most of the time, we play a huge role in the clutter our relationships reflect.

How does your relationship clutter influence your:

Self-Care

Self Growth/Spirituality

Creativity/Life Passion

Intimacy/Significant Other

Family

Community/Friends

Physical Environment/Home

Life Work/Career

Prosperity/Finance

Adventure/Fun

Fitness/Physicality

Vitality/Health

Notes:

FINANCIAL CLUTTER:

How does financial clutter show up in your life?

_____

_____

_____

_____

How do you spend money?

_____

_____

_____

_____

Are your spending habits aligned with your desires, intentions and values?

_____

_____

_____

_____

Are you "reckless" with money?

What are your financial goals? Are they your goals or society's goals?

Describe what saying "Yes!" to financial freedom looks like for you.

Notes:

_____

_____

_____

_____

_____

_____

How does your financial clutter and relationship with or feelings about money influence your:

Self-Care

Self Growth/Spirituality

Creativity/Life Passion

Intimacy/Significant Other

Family

Community/Friends

Physical Environment/Home

Life Work/Career

Prosperity/Finance

Adventure/Fun

Fitness/Physicality

Vitality/Health

Notes:

VITALITY CLUTTER:

How does vitality clutter show up in your life? What choices do you make that might not be aligned with the vitality you want for yourself and your life?

_____

_____

_____

_____

Describe what your version of vitality looks like.

_____

_____

_____

_____

By saying "YES" to your idea of vitality, what steps will you take?

_____

_____

_____

_____

What choices are you willing to take in saying "yes" to vitality?

By default, in saying yes to "vitality", what will you be saying "no" to?

Notes:

How does your vitality clutter influence your:

Self-Care

Self Growth/Spirituality

Creativity/Life Passion

Intimacy/Significant Other

Family

Community/Friends

Physical Environment/Home

Life Work/Career

Prosperity/Finance

Adventure/Fun

Fitness/Physicality

Vitality/Health

Notes:

TIME CLUTTER:

Use time as a metric for where clutter shows up in your life. I'm referring to the time spent doing things which are out of alignment with your highest intentions.

How does time clutter show up in your life?

_____

_____

_____

_____

Do you spend your time the way you'd like to live your life?

_____

_____

_____

_____

Is your time aligned with your intentions and values?

_____

_____

_____

If your experience of time were a landscape, what would it look and feel like? (A freeway during 5 o'clock traffic? A beautiful secluded beach? An ant hill after being stepped on? A stream in the forest?)

My time is spent doing:

Much of the time, I'm thinking about and preoccupied with:

How does time clutter and your relationship with time influence your:

Self-Care

Self Growth/Spirituality

Creativity/Life Passion

Intimacy/Significant Other

Family

Community/Friends

Physical Environment/Home

Life Work/Career

Prosperity/Finance

Adventure/Fun

Fitness/Physicality

Vitality/Health

Notes:

ADDITIONAL CLUTTER QUESTIONS:

List the obstacles in your life blocking access to your intentions and desired outcomes:

I'm saying "YES!" to:

"NO!" to:

What's essential?

Health and Vitality: What's essential?

Relationship and Romance: What's essential?

Financial and Abundance : What's essential?

Work and Career: What's essential?

_____

_____

_____

_____

Fun and Adventure: What's essential?

_____

_____

_____

_____

Friends and Community: What's essential?

_____

_____

_____

_____

Family: What's essential?

_____

_____

_____

_____

Self-Care: What's essential?

_____

_____

_____

_____

Self Knowledge: What's essential?

_____

_____

_____

_____

Home: What's essential?

Physical Environment: What's essential?

Notes:

PERSONAL DECLARATIONS

This is it! Let's declare all you're creating. This is who I am...This is where I'm going...This is how I'm getting there...See yourself through the eyes of your Board of Directors and living your version of a "10" life, describe what you know to be true about yourself, how you live life and where you're heading.

Health & Vitality:

_____

_____

_____

_____

Relationship & Romance:

_____

_____

_____

_____

Prosperity & Abundance:

_____

_____

_____

_____

Life Work & Career:

Fun & Adventure:

Friends & Community:

Family:

Self-Care:

Self Knowledge:

Home:

_____

_____

_____

_____

_____

Physical Environment:

_____

_____

_____

_____

_____

Congratulations! By completing this guide you've made a huge investment toward making your ideal future a reality. When you identify what you want most for your life you're exponentially more likely to achieve it...whatever "it" is. You've taken the first big step toward effective change and creating the life you desire.

The Blueprint for a Self Designed Life was created as a companion guide for the course, yet it offers anyone the opportunity to discover key ingredients for designing their unique version of an ideal life.

If you're interested in taking this process further, visit www.holisticinteriordesign.com for a full listing of courses, products and services.

With love,
Kimberly